Mandy Moore

backstage pass

By Mora Lorrain
and
Amanda Pennychurch

SCHOLASTIC INC.

NEW YORK TORONTO LONDON AUCKLAND SYDNEY MEXICO CITY NEW DELHI HONG KONG

Photography Credits:

Front cover: Joseph Galea; back cover: Joseph Galea; page 4: Joseph Galea; page 5, left: Joseph Galea; page 5, right: Joseph Galea; page 8: Barry Talesnick/Retna; page 9: Barry Talesnick/Retna; page 10: Barry Talesnick/Retna; page 12: Joseph Galea; page 13: Joseph Galea; page 15: Bill Davila/Retna; page 16: Joseph Galea; page 17: Joseph Galea; page 18: Joseph Galea; page 19: Joseph Galea; page 20: Steve Granitz/Retna; page 21:Joseph Galea; page 22: Barry Talesnick/Retna; page 23, top: Joseph Galea; page 23, bottom: Gilbert Flores/Celebrity Photo Agency; pages 24-25: Joseph Galea; page 26: Robin Platzer Twin Images; page 27, top: Joseph Galea; page 27, bottom: Gilbert Flores/Celebrity Photo Agency; page 30: Joseph Galea; page 31: Joseph Galea; page 33: Joseph Galea; page 35: Joseph Galea; page 36: Joseph Galea; page 37: Joseph Galea; page 38: Joseph Galea; page 39: Bernhard Kuhmstedt/Retna; page 40: Bernhard Kuhmstedt/Retna; page 41, top: Bill Davila/Retna; page 41, bottom: Bill Davila/Retna; page 42, top: Bill Davila/Retna; page 42, bottom: Bill Davila/Retna; page 43, left: Robin Platzer Twin Images; page 43, right: Joseph Galea; page 44, left: Tara Canova/Retna; page 44, right: Joseph Galea.

ISBN 0-439-22223-0

Copyright © 2000 by Scholastic Inc.

All rights reserved. Published by Scholastic Inc., 555 Broadway, New York, NY 10012.

SCHOLASTIC and associated logos are trademarks and/or registered trademarks of Scholastic Inc.

12 11 10 9 8 7 6 5 4 3 2   0 1 2 3 4 5/0

Printed in the U.S.A.

First Scholastic printing, October 2000

GUIDE TO WHAT'S INSIDE

Introduction

When Mandy Moore, whose first single, "Candy," went gold, became successful back in 1999, people were pretty impressed. She had a polished voice and an amazing musical range. She had lots of charm and a great attitude. And she seemed to be able to do anything she set her mind to — she was a pro on the screen, in the studio, and before a crowd. But the thing that really seemed to blow people away was how young she was. With the release of her album *So Real* at the tender age of fifteen, Mandy achieved the kind of success some folks wait their whole lives to find. How could this new kid be *so good so quick?*

Mandy Moore — just your regular, everyday, All-American pop star.

Well, if you ask Mandy, she'll put a different spin on it. She may be young, but she's *no* new kid. By the time *So Real* was released, she was a seasoned performer. She had already been working as a singer for five years, and was doing everything to prepare for her big break — she performed at sporting events, sang in musical theater productions, even appeared in commercials. For Mandy had been dreaming about a life in showbiz. "I always knew," she says, "ever since I was really little, like, about when I was six. I knew that I wanted to be an entertainer." Do the math. Mandy may have made it when she was fifteen, but she had been working up to her success for a long time. Like, nine years!

Still, lots of six-year-old girls dream of being a star. What makes Mandy Moore's story different? Read on! You're about to find out.

What
a
cutie!

Sometimes meeting and greeting fans takes hours — but Mandy loves it.

Chapter 1

Meet Mandy

THE BEGINNING

Amanda Leigh Moore was born on April 10, 1984, in Nashua, New Hampshire. When she was only two months old, her family moved to Orlando, Florida. She has lived there ever since.

Orlando is a great place to be if you want to make it in the music biz. Just ask 'N Sync, Backstreet Boys, and Britney Spears — they all got started there. But Mandy's family was not in Orlando for the music scene. And Mandy definitely didn't grow up as an "O-Town insider." She was just a kid who really loved music.

Sure, Mandy is totally down-to-earth. But she was still thrilled when her first album came out.

When she was six, Mandy saw her first musical play — a performance of *Oklahoma!* From that day on, she was hooked on the idea of becoming a singer. She spent lots of time just "jumping on my bed and singing," and would walk around her house belting out tunes from *The Little Mermaid.*

Still, Mandy was young — and her family didn't take her musical aspirations too seriously. Her younger brother, Kyle, and her older brother, Scott, were too busy with sports to think about music. And Mandy's parents, Don and Stacy, thought that her singing was cute, but just a phase.

Only this phase didn't seem to be passing.

THE LESSONS

After three years of hearing Mandy do Madonna and *Little Mermaid* renditions, Don and Stacy realized this whole singing thing was here to stay. They didn't have much choice. By age nine, Mandy was driving them crazy, bugging them for singing and dancing lessons every chance she got. And she wasn't taking no for an answer. Mandy explains, "They were like 'OK, we think you're old enough; we'll get you some voice lessons to make sure you're breathing properly and singing from your diaphragm and all that good stuff.'"

After her parents gave in, Mandy enrolled in just about every class a young performer can take. She learned to sing and act and was devoted to her tap dancing lessons. Through the years, she did all this on top of a busy school schedule. Not only was she working hard as a cheerleader for Pop Warner Football, she became an honor student at Rock Lake middle school in Altamonte Springs, Florida. As she told MTV, "I actually liked school when I was in school. I was a weird kid, I guess."

The best thing Mandy did for her career was go to musical theater summer camp. She had wanted to be in a professional play

Most people get shy in front of a camera. Not Mandy! It's where she's most comfortable.

7

Looking good takes lots of time . . .

ever since seeing that *Oklahoma!* performance, and the musical theater camp gave her a taste of life on the stage. More important, it helped her land her first real singing role — Ngana in a local production of the musical *South Pacific.* After that, she appeared in over a dozen more musicals in the central Florida area, and had leads in *Bye Bye Birdie* and *Guys and Dolls.*

It seemed like all the training was paying off. Mandy was loving every minute. But it was also getting a little more serious. How far did she really want to take this whole singing thing?

"OH, SAY CAN YOU SEE . . ."

As much as she loved musicals, the theater was not Mandy's only performing arena. New doors were beginning to open, and she took advantage of everything that came her way.

One of the best opportunities came via the sports industry in Orlando. She won a local singing contest and got to perform the "Star-Spangled Banner" for Chris Evert's Pro-Celebrity Tennis Tournament. Then, as she told *MXG*, "I sent a tape of myself singing the national anthem to the Orlando Magic, and they liked it. So I got to sing in front of eighteen thousand people. After that it was a domino effect.

. . . Sometimes it can take an entire morning . . .

Every sports team in Orlando was like, 'Hey, you're that little girl that sang the anthem . . . Do you want to do it for us?' And I ended up doing it like a hundred times that year . . ." It was just a matter of time before she became known as "the national anthem girl."

Soon Mandy could barely keep up with her busy singing schedule. She got tons of small jobs around town, including lots of work in advertising. She was singing jingles, doing voiceovers, and even acting in commercials for companies like Chevrolet Cars, Cadbury Chocolate, Kmart, and Epcot Center. She was simply taking her own advice: "Life will give you opportunities that you should not pass up. Take advantage of every opportunity you can."

What Mandy didn't know was that she was about to be handed the biggest opportunity of her life.

A BIG BREAK

When Mandy was thirteen, she landed a job singing the

theme song for a local TV show. One of the producers working on the project liked what he heard and invited Mandy to come to TransContinental Studios (home of BSB, 'N Sync, LFO) to make a "demo" — a recording that aspiring singers send to music execs when trying to get a record deal. It was a lucky break, but a small one. Normally, a demo is the first step in a long process of getting a record contract. (Just ask any one of the millions of struggling songwriters out there!)

In the studio, however, Mandy got a second lucky break. A talent scout heard her and was floored by her voice. He quickly sent her unfinished tape to a few friends in the music biz. "He didn't even tell me he was doing it," she said. Before long, three major labels were offering her deals.

Of course, Mandy had to do some hard thinking about all this. She was still pretty young, and this was a big step. And if Mandy was ready to take it, there was still the question of her, uuhhhh, parents. When she first started getting offers, she explained, they "were kind of hesitant, because really, you have to sacrifice a lot, and people sometimes forget that." But that changed. Mandy describes, "They knew how much I loved it, and how much I really wanted to give it my all and try. I'm really grateful that they were that supportive."

In the end, Mandy signed with Sony's record division, *550* ("because they're the best"). She had landed a major record deal and was only thirteen years old!

Now she had some serious work to do. Like, she had to make a record. And she had to promote it. And she had to go on tour. Still, it was all part of Mandy's dream. And she was ready to run with it.

GOING FOR THE DREAM

As soon as the contracts were signed, Mandy went back to the recording studio. But this time it was the real deal. Not a demo. *A real album.*

Mandy worked hard with producers to develop her own style and sound. She didn't write the songs on *So Real*, but she spent long hours with the songwriters, telling them what she wanted

the songs to be about, and to sound like. Mandy had lots of influences: Whitney Houston, Natalie Imbruglia, Mariah Carey, Bette Midler, Madonna, to name a few. But she also had her own ideas. The end result on *So Real* was a sound that was totally unique and totally Mandy. "My music's kinda different from what's out there right now," she says. "It's pop, but my songs have a little more rock and a little more R&B in 'em."

Still, what happens in the studio is different from what happens in performance. And even before her album and singles were released, Mandy had to face the fans — live and onstage. It was her biggest test yet, but the challenge thrilled her. And she was lucky enough to land two pretty sweet gigs — opening act for a leg of 'N Sync's 1999 summer tour *and then* opening for part of the Backstreet Boys' fall tour.

How cool was that? As you can imagine, touring with the world's two hottest boy bands was a

When Mandy's onstage, she gives it everything she's got.

dream come true for fifteen-year-old Mandy. She loved working with 'N Sync and said she "learned everything from them." And she felt the same way about BSB: "The guys are so sweet. They are really down-to-earth, and that makes touring with them fun. Plus they are true entertainers and put on a great show."

But touring wasn't just about Mandy hanging out with the boys. She was, after all, one of the tour's stars. And for the first time in her life, she was finding out what it was like to be famous. The crowds went crazy for her when she performed. Especially when she sang "Candy" — a real crowd pleaser. She spent hours before and after every show signing autographs and meeting fans. Everybody seemed to be into Mandy, who was now being called the "Candy Girl!" And when "Candy" was released right after the 'N Sync tour ended, it was an overnight hit. It sold over 500,000 copies and the video became a mainstay on MTV's *Total Request Live.* In

Okay . . .
No one looks
this good in front
of the camera!

fact, "Candy" did better than anyone expected — so much so that Sony decided to push forward the release date of her *So Real* album. Rather than releasing it in 2000, Sony put it out in December 1999, right after her tour with BSB ended. People wanted more of the Candy Girl, and they didn't want to wait.

YOU, GO! CANDY GIRL!

So now Mandy had two major tours behind her and a brand-new album on its way to selling about a million copies. Time to sit back and enjoy the ride, right? No way. Mandy's only question was, "What's next?" Her answer was to go after as many opportunities as she could.

First came MTV. She was already a regular guest VJ on MTV's *TRL*, but wondered if she could expand her role there. MTV totally thought so — they signed her to a three-year deal to appear on some of their other shows, including *FANatic*, *Summer Beach House*, *Snowed In*, *Spring Break 2000*, *Rock 'N' Jock*, and *Fashionably Loud*. Currently Mandy's developing a show of her own there.

She was also signed up by cosmetic company Neutrogena. She's their new global spokeswoman — because of her perfect skin, no doubt. And she's a model for Tommy Hilfiger and Wet Seal. And she's appeared on several TV shows: *Roswell*, *Dawson's Creek*, *Donnie and Marie*, and *The Tonight Show*, to name a few. And she's doing all this while touring all over the world, learning to play the guitar, and writing new songs.

Sound like enough? Maybe for most people. But Mandy has no plans to slow down. She says, "The more people get to know me as a full personality, the better my chances are of being viewed as more than just another teen flash in the pan. I plan to be like Madonna, reinventing myself and making records for a long time to come."

Mandy is very down-to-earth, smart, kind, and generous. She hasn't let the music industry change any of that. She's finishing high school with a tutor, but she's still very close with her old school friends. Her family is always around (even if it means touring with her). And she spends as much time at home as possible. Most of all, she keeps everything in perspective and remains grateful for all she's accomplished. As she says, "I don't feel I've missed out on anything about growing up because I feel so fortunate. There are so many kids that would love to be doing what I'm doing."

Stardom has changed Mandy's life, but it hasn't changed her. In lots of ways, she's just like anyone else. She needs to relax, have fun, and be with people who really care about her. Check out what Mandy's all about when she's not being a famous teen sensation.

"I wanna be with you."

15

Chapter 2 Mandy Offstage

MANDY'S FAM

Mandy's parents are nothing like "stereotypical" stage parents. They never pushed her into the music industry and just want her to be happy. They're also kind of protective. Mom Stacy Moore usually travels with her when she's on tour. And sometimes Dad Don, does too — when he can get away from his job as an airline pilot. But although her parents are always with Mandy, they try not to get too absorbed in her career. "I am her mother," her mom firmly told one interviewer when he asked if she was Mandy's business manager.

Mandy is also close with her brothers. When

Mandy's a total pro. But she also likes to kick back and relax.

asked about how they've all gotten along since Mandy's career took off, she said: "They're still the same, like my older brother [Scott — nineteen] is real protective. They love hangin' out at MTV and stuff. They're really great about it, and since my dad is a pilot, they get to fly up and see me." Mandy has also been using her younger brother, Kyle, (fourteen) in her videos. Maybe they'll do a duet one day, if Kyle stops thinking about sports long enough.

Any pets? Mandy has three cats — Milo, Chloe, and Zoe. And there might be more to come. If Mandy's parents let her, she'll be getting a new kitten.

From high-school freshman to teen megastar. Mandy's handled the whole trip with poise and grace.

MANDY'S FRIENDS

Mandy's friends are important to her, and she makes sure she spends time with them. When asked about an upcoming holiday, she said she was planning "just to get home and spend some time with my friends and my family. I get to drive around, because all my friends are turning sixteen now. We can drive by ourselves, so I'm looking forward to that."

But friendships can be hard to make (and hard to keep) when you're the newly crowned Princess of Pop. Still, she tries. "I look for someone who's really open, someone I can talk to and that I can trust. I like someone who likes me for who I am and not because I'm recording and acting, someone who's supportive, and who will still be my friend when I get home."

No question that friends and family are number one in Mandy's life.

How'd you like to have these guys backing you up?

SCHOOL

Singing stars still have to do their homework, albeit sometimes on a slightly different schedule. "I'm tutored," Mandy told MTV. "I actually go through Texas Tech University, the extended studies program. I just get my books and my curriculum, and I do most of my work by myself on the road. When I go home I check it with a tutor. I can get a chapter done in an hour and a half, or two hours, and just move on to the next thing."

While that may sound like a recipe for slacking off, Mandy's super serious about academics. And while the Texas Tech program is the right thing for right now, part of Mandy misses the old days. She loved school, and totally gets how important it is.

MANDY'S STUFF

Being a performer means getting to do more than most of your peers. Mandy's life is mostly different when she's on the road: She stays in lots of really cool hotels (no Motel 6!), hangs out with other celebs, rides everywhere in limos and, oh yeah, works really, really, *really* hard.

But when Mandy's at home, she's pretty much like any other kid. She doesn't have a maid or a limo or a gold-plated toothbrush. In fact, her stuff is a lot like any other teen girl's. "I have a lot of Broadway stage play posters up in my room," she says, "because I really like Broadway. I have my CD player, of course, and my TV, my phone, 'cause I can't live without my phone! And my computer, because I'm always on-line."

But what about the really important stuff? "I like a big purse. My purse is made by Steve Madden. I carry a lot of stuff. I always carry a brush, and now I carry my cell phone, which is purple — they didn't have a pink phone. I always carry powder, and some form of glitter, and my wallet. And I always have lip gloss, a real natural light pink color. Plus, gum and antibacterial gel."

Still, as normal as Mandy's off-stage life is, she allows herself to fantasize about few luxuries: "I know that Justin Timberlake [of 'N Sync] has a Mercedes SUV and I would kind of like one of those, too. I want a silver one. Whether I get that or not, it's up to my mom and my dad. To say I have the same car as Justin is pretty cool."

Mandy at the 1999 Billboard Music Awards

KICKIN' BACK

Mandy may work way more than an average teen, but she likes to chill out just like everyone else.

Here's one of her favorite ways to veg: "I love a bubble bath and scented candles. I light a bunch of vanilla-scented candles. And also, I have these little oil things that you rub on your pressure points. It makes you calm down."

Another way that Mandy copes with her crazy schedule is by keeping a journal. It allows her to take a few minutes out of her busy life to think about where she is and where she's going. She said, "My parents were like, Mandy, you have to keep a journal on the road, otherwise you're going to totally forget all the experiences and stuff a year from now. And I started thinking about that, and I really wanted to have this — just for me, starting out, my first tour. I wanted to have everything documented and later on in life I can go, 'Look how stupid I was!' Something like that."

Mandy taking a few minutes to relax

Chapter 3

Mandy on Her Music

Buzz. There's a whole lot of it going around about Mandy. Everyone seems to have an opinion about her — especially regarding her music. But there's nothing quite like hearing about the Mandy-sound from the girl herself. Check out some of the things she has to say about her career and her music.

WHO ARE MANDY'S FAVORITE MALE SINGERS?

"I really like Jordan Knight," she said to an interviewer at *TeenBeat.* "But I also like all the boy groups, like 98°, 'N Sync, and Backstreet Boys."

WHAT'S IT LIKE TO HEAR "CANDY" ON THE RADIO?

"It is the trippiest thing in the whole world just to [hear] 'And here's "Candy" by Mandy Moore,'" Mandy said in an interview with MTV. "It's like, oh my gosh, it's a feeling you can never get used to. And it's a feeling that's so indescribable. You know, I did the CD and I knew 'Candy' was going to probably be the first single, but it's still like [I thought], maybe it will be played by a few radio stations and sell a couple [copies] and stuff. It went gold . . . and I just freaked out!"

MANDY ON FRIENDSHIP AND STARDOM:

"When I first started recording, it was hard. My friends didn't understand why I couldn't hang out with them as much.

These days, Mandy has a lot to smile about.

I thought they'd talk behind my back or be jealous, but they've become really supportive."

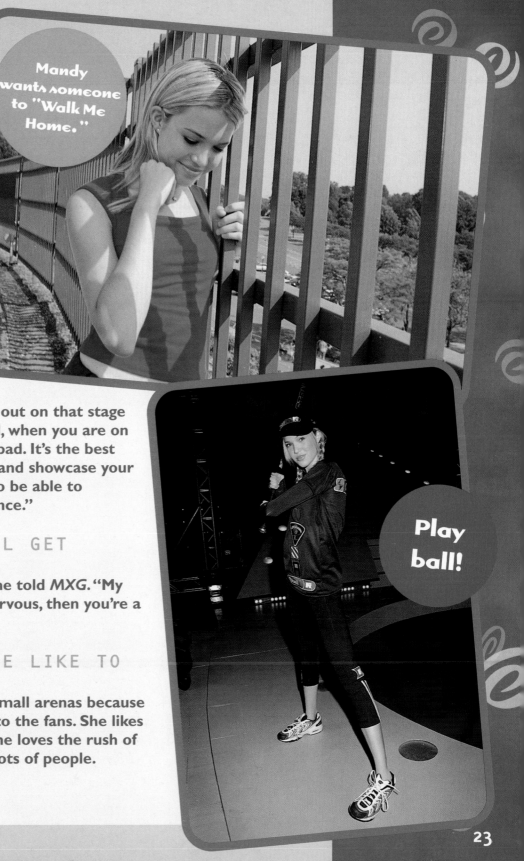

Mandy wants someone to "Walk Me Home."

Play ball!

WHAT'S THE BEST?
"For me the best part is just being a performer. Just being able to get out there, no matter how crappy your day has been. Being able to get out on that stage every night, guaranteed, when you are on a tour. Nothing can be bad. It's the best feeling to go out there and showcase your music for people, and to be able to connect with the audience."

DOES SHE STILL GET NERVOUS?
"Before every show," she told MXG. "My thing is, if you're not nervous, then you're a little bit too cocky."

WHERE DOES SHE LIKE TO PERFORM?
Everywhere. She likes small arenas because they let her get closer to the fans. She likes big stadiums because she loves the rush of performing in front of lots of people.

Mandy Moore

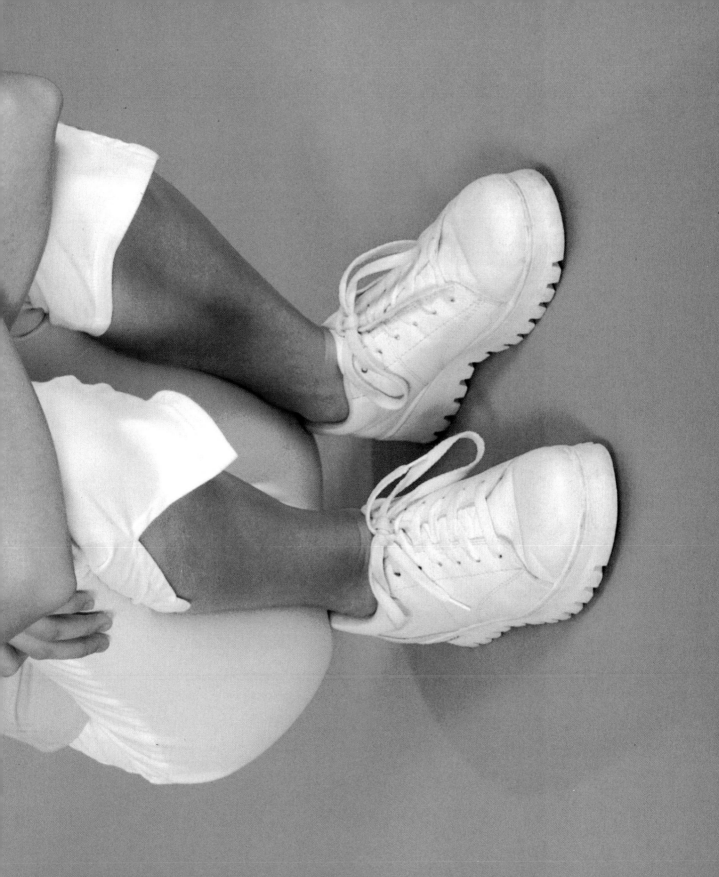

WHAT ARE MANDY'S GOALS?

"I am just going to do my own thing and I am just going to try and grow with my career and strive for longevity," she told a fan in a Yahoo chat. "Just to be kinda different. My goal is to stay in the business for as long as I can."

ADVICE FOR ASPIRING SUPERSTARS:

"Keep up what they are doing. Don't listen to the mean comments that people say. Have confidence and you can go far in life and accomplish what you want. Never ever pass up good opportunities."

You just have to say it again . . . "She's such a cutie!"

WHAT'S MANDY'S FAVORITE SONG TO PERFORM?

Mandy loves to do "So Real." It's usually the first song she sings when she's giving a concert.

MANDY'S BIGGEST INFLUENCE:

"My grandmother, I think. At least that's where my talent probably comes from. She was a dancer in the theater district of London, the West End."

MANDY ON TOURING:

She told teenvoice.com, "You're never in one city for more than a few days, so it's really cool. Whenever you're there you can try to soak up everything you can, to just experience everything ."

MANDY ON DANCING:

"My whole philosophy is, I want be known as a singer who can dance

Mandy is "What You Want."

and not a dancer who can sing," she told MTV. "My stage show is more based around the singing, because I have four incredible guy dancers who are backing me up and just busting their butts every night. They're doing a wonderful job, and the audience really likes that, so they're really receptive to that."

WHAT'S LIFE LIKE ON THE ROAD?

In a Yahoo chat, Mandy said, "I miss my family and friends so much. I am lucky that my mom travels with me and sometimes my dad does, too. I travel with my computer and chat with them, but I miss my friends and family."

Check out that smile. No wonder Mandy was chosen as one of the "25 Hottest Stars Under 25" by Teen People.

Chapter 4

"Moore" About Mandy

Think you know everything there is to know about the "Candy" girl? Think again! Here — in no particular order — are all the facts *and stats* about the amazin' Mandy.

FULL NAME: **Amanda Leigh Moore**

NICKNAME: **Mandy**

BIRTHDATE: **April 10, 1984**

ZODIAC SIGN: **Aries — *the Ram***

BIRTHPLACE: **Nashua, New Hampshire**

LIVES NOW: **Orlando, Florida**

HEIGHT: **5'9"**

EYES: **Hazel**

HAIR: **Blond**

SHOE SIZE: **10**

MOM & DAD: **Stacy and Don**

BROTHERS: **Scott, 19, and Kyle, 14**

SISTERS: **None**

BEST FRIEND: **Bonnie**

Mandy works "eighteen to twent_ hour days, day aft_ day after day. It'_ incredibly amazing and I love it, but it's tiring."

FIRST RECORDING: "The Star-Spangled Banner"

BEST PLACE TO DANCE: At a BSB concert

FAVORITE BOOK: *A Land Remembered*

FAVORITE MOVIE: *Beaches*

FAVORITE ACTOR: Ryan Phillippe

FAVORITE ACTRESS: Gwyneth Paltrow

MOST LIKELY TO SHOP AT: Guess?, Diesel

FAVORITE VIDEO: *Waiting for Tonight* by Jennifer Lopez

FAVORITE SINGERS: Whitney Houston, Madonna, Bette Midler

PETS: Three cats — Milo, Chloe, Zoe

FAVORITE FOOD: Cotton candy — pink, of course!

MOST EMBARRASSING MOMENT: Breaking a heel during a homecoming photo-op

CITY SHE'D MOVE TO: New York

STAYS IN SHAPE BY: Sit-ups . . . and saying NO to fast food!

HERO AS A LITTLE GIRL: Madonna (and still is!)

FAVE PASTIMES: When not shopping — she's hangin' with friends

TV SHOWS MOST LIKELY TO WATCH: MTVs *Real World*

LAST SCHOOL ATTENDED: Rock Lake Middle School in Altamonte Springs, FL

DRIVING YET? Nope, just a learner's permit

STICK SHIFT OR AUTOMATIC: Automatic

DREAM MACHINE: Mercedes SUV

SPORTS PLAYED: Lacrosse

BIGGEST HOBBY: Surfin' the Internet

FAVORITE EXPRESSION: Beat! (as in cool)

LOVE TO TRADE PLACES WITH: Janeane Garafalo (actress)

PET PEEVES: Smoking ("gross"), nail biting ("I'm trying to stop"), and chipped nail polish

BEST SUBJECTS: English and French

WORST SUBJECTS: Math (but she's trying!)

FIRST ACTING GIG: Ngana in a local production of *South Pacific*

EVER A CHEERLEADER? Yep, Pop Warner Football

MAKEUP COLOR? Baby pinks. "It matches all my clothes."

HAIR CARE: "I use Biolage, and Herbal Essence is cool."

FREE TIME ACTIVITIES: Shopping ("Of, course!"), writing in her journal, and movies

FAVE LAZY-DAY ACTIVITY: Just hanging out with friends

FAVORITE ANIMAL: Monkey

FAVORITE CARTOON: *Daria*

FAVORITE ICE CREAM: Peanut-butter cup

Mandy on Stardom: "I want to always be happy and have fun with it. I don't want to be in a position where it's not fun."

FAVORITE
TOOTHPASTE:
**Arm and
Hammer
Advance White**

GREATEST
FEAR: **Losing
someone she loves**

TYPICAL
BREAKFAST:
**Bagel (never
cereal)**

WHAT'S IN HER
PURSE? **Brush, cell
phone, lip gloss,
wallet**

WHAT'S IN HER
BEDROOM?
**Broadway posters,
CD player, TV, and a
computer**

CELEB CRUSHES:
**Justin Timberlake,
Jordan Knight, Joey
McIntyre**

SHE'D LUV TO
DATE: **Carson Daly**

PHILOSOPHY OF
LIFE: **"Take one day
at a time!"**

ASK MANDY
**Q: How would *you*
describe yourself?**

**A: I'm really honest,
sensitive, and funky.**

*"Sometimes
it annoys me
when people judge
me before they meet
me and get a
feel for what
I'm like."*

Chapter 5 Mandy on Boys

No question, Mandy Moore is a *mega-boy-magnet*. But being a singer doesn't mean that romance is any easier. Sometimes, just the opposite is true. You never know if a boy likes you *or your fame*. And being asked out by every guy in sight doesn't really get you anywhere. Whom do you trust? Major hotties often turn out to be major losers. And it's not easy having a boyfriend when you're on the road so much. . . . You never ever get to see each other.

So how does Mandy handle the guy thing? Here are some of her secrets:

1. BE SMART. Make sure he's interested for the right reasons. Mandy looks for a guy who likes her for her, not for her fame.

2. BE BRAVE. Don't be afraid to ask a guy out. He'll probably like it.

3. BE STRONG. If a guy breaks up with you, don't let it get you down. Be thankful for the things you have. As Mandy told *J-14* magazine, the best thing for dealing with a breakup is, "Being with friends who love you for you."

4. BE HONEST. Always trust your instincts — you'll know when it's the real thing. And, by the way, Mandy definitely believes in love at first sight.

5. BE SLY. If you see a guy you like but don't really know him, find a clever way to break the ice.

6. BE TRUE TO YOURSELF. Know what you want. Mandy wants a guy who doesn't play games.

FACT OR FICTION?
So who is Mandy's boyfriend? Right now, no one. Why? *NO TIME.* She hardly even has time to see her friends and family.

Still, people like to talk. And the down side to fame is dealing with gossip. The most widespread stories are about her dating members of the O-Town boy bands like 'N Sync and Backstreet Boys. Fact: these stories are ALL FALSE (especially the one about Nick Carter).

But Mandy has learned to be good-natured about the stories. Mostly, she just blows them off. She told *J-14* magazine, "It makes me laugh when I hear rumors like that about me and people I'm just friends with, or I've never even met before."

Occasionally, however, Mandy will 'fess up to a crush: "I had a little crush on Ryan Phillippe," she said in a Yahoo chat. "I know he has a wife and child, but I have a crush on him all the same."

So Mandy is single. This is good news for all the guys who *have it bad* for Mandy (and that's a lot of guys). The bad news is that it doesn't look like she's slowing down her schedule anytime soon — so she's probably not on the lookout for a full-time beau.

Does Mandy have a boyfriend? No one major . . . yet!

Writing songs for any album is a difficult process. And while Mandy didn't compose the songs on *So Real*, she spent a long time working with the producers and songwriters to make sure the music reflected her taste and her ideas. The result was an album that combined the sharp edge of a professional production with the honesty of Mandy's fifteen-year-old outlook. As Mandy says, "Some of it is my life. Some of it I haven't experienced. But I was really careful to make sure that everything I was singing about is believable for a fifteen-year-old."

The result is that Mandy's music is uniquely Mandy. But what is she really saying in her songs? What is her message? And what are fans saying on her Web site? Check out the *So Real* song guide below.

TITLE: "So Real"
WHAT'S IT ABOUT: Like the title says . . . her love for this boy is real.
THE MANDY MESSAGE: Don't rush. Be yourself.
WHAT THE FANS ARE SAYING: "feels like a rock song" "great groove"

TITLE: "Candy"
WHAT'S IT ABOUT: No doubt about it, boys are oh-so-sweet.

"[My] record company is the best. They let me be me."

THE MANDY MESSAGE: They're not all jerks.
WHAT THE FANS ARE SAYING: "absolute favorite"
"amazing hook" "loved it ever since I first heard it"

TITLE: "**What You Want**"
WHAT'S IT ABOUT: This love is the real thing. Don't blow it!
THE MANDY MESSAGE: Ask for what you want.
WHAT THE FANS ARE SAYING: "slow . . . but still
danceable" "the guitar reminds
me of Natalie Imbruglia"
"moody!"

TITLE: "**Walk Me Home**"
WHAT'S IT ABOUT: She
wants to know — will you
(could you) be my boyfriend?
THE MANDY MESSAGE:
You don't always know if he
likes you.
WHAT THE FANS ARE
SAYING: "totally sweet"
"I love her voice on this
one — it's great" "kind of
like an R&B song"

TITLE: "**Lock Me in
Your Heart**"
WHAT'S IT ABOUT:
There must be a place
where our love can work.
THE MANDY
MESSAGE: Yes, yes, yes
— believe in love.
WHAT THE FANS
ARE SAYING: "I have
a dream lover, too. I
know how she feels"
"Her voice in the
background sounds
cool"

"There are long days of hard work, but it's been quite a journey for me."

35

TITLE: "Telephone"

TITLE: "Quit Breaking My Heart"
WHAT'S IT ABOUT: Warning: Love can hurt.
THE MANDY MESSAGE: Be strong.
WHAT THE FANS ARE SAYING: "really pretty" "I can relate to it!" "I'm going to play it for my jerky boyfriend"

TITLE: "Let Me Be the One"
WHAT'S IT ABOUT: All she wants . . . is to get back with the b-friend.
THE MANDY MESSAGE: Keep hope alive.
WHAT THE FANS ARE SAYING: "funky" "great dance beat"

TITLE: "Not Too Young"
WHAT'S IT ABOUT: She's not too young to do the right thing.
THE MANDY MESSAGE: You go, girl!
WHAT THE FANS ARE SAYING: "got a great TLC sound" "I get it!" "thunder is a great effect"

Mandy may pout for the camera. But in real life, she's usually pretty cheerful.

TITLE: "**Love Shot**"
WHAT'S IT ABOUT: Look out . . . she's got a powerful love to share.
THE MANDY MESSAGE: You better warn him!
WHAT THE FANS ARE SAYING: "this could be a single" "Mandy's voice rules"

TITLE: "**I Like It**"
WHAT'S IT ABOUT: It's all about us being together.
THE MANDY MESSAGE: Listen to him.
WHAT THE FANS ARE SAYING: "sounds like a club song" "I had to call my boyfriend"

TITLE: "**Love for You Always**"
WHAT'S IT ABOUT: He makes it all worthwhile.
THE MANDY MESSAGE: Love him!
WHAT THE FANS ARE SAYING: "great lyrics" "I like the way the tempo changes" "I like singing along with this song"

The question on everyone's mind: Who's the one for Mandy?

Mandy's talent is "So Real."

Part of the fun of being a celeb is hanging out with other celebs. Mandy's had her fair share of "star encounters." Some are her friends, some are her heroes, and some she met because they were fans of her work. One thing's for sure, Mandy is lovin' her life among the stars.

THE BOY BANDS

One thing really makes Mandy the envy of every music lovin' pop girl: In the span of seven months, in the last year of the twentieth century, she got to go on tour with both 'N Sync *and* the Backstreet Boys. How cool was that?

And when people ask her about the experience she is all too happy to share it. This is how she described one of her first meetings with 'N Sync: "I was kind of **sweating meeting my favorite** guy in 'N Sync, J.C. Chasez — love him. He listened to my music and he liked it and he was just a sweet guy."

That helped Mandy get over her nerves. And throughout both tours she developed much deeper relationships with the members of those bands — both as professionals and friends.

"They're almost inspirational to me," Mandy said while talking about 'N Sync and BSB to an MTV interviewer. " . . . They are so genuine, and they are so real, and it seems that nothing has fazed them. All the success they've had hasn't changed them a bit. That's something I really look up to. I think sometimes [when you

Mandy's first big tour was with 'N Sync. She says they taught her a lot.

Mandy says the Backstreet Boys are totally sweet and down-to-earth.

become famous] you don't stay grounded, and you forget who you really are, and you start to be, like, someone you're not. But those guys are the exact opposite of that. They are so cool, and they're so supportive. They come out and watch my show [and say things like], 'Good job, is there anything we can get for you?' So I really felt like I was part of the tour, and it was such an honor to be there. We just had so much fun."

HEROS

Mandy is the first to give props to her role models. She usually places Madonna at the top of the list, but there are many other performers who have influenced her. They include Jessica Simpson, Mariah Carey, Whitney Houston, Celine Dion, Bette Midler, Janet Jackson, Britney Spears, and Natalie Imbruglia. Part of the thrill of Mandy's skyrocketing career has been meeting some of these people.

"I remember being speechless when I met Celine Dion. She is so amazing! I think that is the first time I have not been able to speak in my life," she admitted. That may have been the first

"I'm definitely starstruck by everybody. I feel like a fan."

time. But it wasn't the last. She was just as floored when she met Janet Jackson.

Of course, meeting megastars starts to get to be a normal occurrence when you are one yourself. But Mandy's not likely to get bored by it. "I love to meet everyone I can," she says. "Each person brings a unique lifestyle to the table."

Perhaps the most exciting thing about Mandy's success is that she's now a role model for other aspiring singers. There are millions of girls who look up to her the way she looked up to Madonna and Janet Jackson. And in a few years a new generation of young pop stars will no doubt list her as a major influence.

Did MTV luck out, or what???

MTV

MTV studios may be the headquarters of a powerful music empire, but it's also just a cool place to go and hang out — if they let you in the front door, that is. But getting in hasn't been a problem for Mandy. And these days, she's

How did Mandy become such a big star? Her fans called every radio station in America and demanded to hear her music.

just one of the gang — hangin' at MTV studios not only when she's working on a show, but also when she feels like kicking back and socializing.

Mandy is very down-to-earth about it all. When she talks about her time at MTV, she's quick to point out how fortunate she is to have the network's support. But the folks at MTV look at it

Mandy's great onstage for one reason: She loves every minute of it.

No wonder she's the new Neutrogena model.

from another point of view: They're pretty lucky to have her. In fact, the relationship has been so great that it looks like it'll continue for a long time to come. Or at least for the next three years, which is the length of Mandy's sweet new MTV contract. And MTV is definitely keeping Mandy busy with her spots on *FANatic*, *Summer Beach House*, *Snowed In*, *Spring Break 2000*, etc., etc., etc.

People compare Britney Spears to Mandy, but these two girls have completely different sounds.

Mandy doesn't mind the comparisons to other teen stars. She's just happy to be in their company.

But despite all the new stuff she'll never stop droppin' in on the *TRL* set. She can't give that up. She loves to chill out, play videos, and talk to fans. And there's one other thing she's kinda into — hangin' with major hottie supreme Carson Daly. But who wouldn't be?

MANDY AND BRITNEY

When Mandy first exploded on the scene, there was a lot of talk about her being "the newest, latest cute blond singer." She was quickly compared to other teen sensations like Jessica Simpson and Christina Aguilera. Most people, however, compared Mandy with the super teen singing queen, Britney Spears.

The two have a lot of respect for each other. And both believe that's there room for each of them — and others — at the top of the charts. Hey! If there's room for 'N Sync, the Backstreet Boys, LFO, 98°, Hanson, etc. there's room for Mandy and Britney, and all the other talented teens.

But in case you're interested . . . check out this chart that compares the two amazing divas!

	MANDY	BRITNEY
FULL NAME	Amanda Leigh Moore	Britney Jean Spears
BORN	4/10/84	12/2/81
FIRST SINGLE	"Candy" (8/17/99)	" . . . Baby One More Time" (1/12/99)
FIRST SOLO GIG	Singing the national anthem at sporting events	Singing tour of American malls
BIG BREAK	Being discovered while singing a demo	Played an "evil child" in an off-Broadway play — later became a Mousketeer
RECORD LABEL	Epic/550	Jive Records
FIRST OPENED FOR	'N Sync	Backstreet Boys
WRITES OWN LYRICS	Not yet	Wrote one song on recently released album
INSPIRATIONS	Madonna, Bette Midler	Barbra Streisand, Whitney Houston
WOULD LIKE TO DO A DUET WITH	Madonna	Ricky Martin
INSTRUMENTS PLAYED	Guitar	None
BIG $$$ ENDORSEMENTS	Neutrogena	Tommy Hilfiger
FALLBACK CAREER	Photo-journalist	Dance teacher

Chapter 8

Discography and Stuff

RECORD LABEL:	Epic/550
DEBUT CD:	*So Real*
FIRST SINGLE:	"Candy"
FIRST VIDEO:	"Candy"
SECOND SINGLE:	"Walk Me Home"
SECOND VIDEO:	"Walk Me Home"
THIRD SINGLE:	"I Wanna Be With You"
THIRD VIDEO:	"I Wanna Be With You"

There are also several dance remixes of Mandy's songs. You can't buy them. But you can find some of them on Mandy's official Web site (mandymoore.com)

For lyrics to Mandy's music, check out gurlpages.com/music/mandymoore/lyrics.html

Candy Single CD Tracks:

01: Candy [Album Version]

02: Candy [Instrumental]

03: Snippets: So Real/What You Want/ Lock Me in Your Heart/Quit Breaking My Heart

The Candy Single CD also contains a free limited-edition poster and behind the scenes footage of the Candy Video.

KEEPIN' UP WITH MANDY

Madonna may be the "Material Girl," but Mandy is on her way to becoming the "Media Girl." Here are the best ways for keeping up with Mandy:

INTERNET

The best way to stay up to date with Mandy is in cyberspace. As she says, "I'm on [it] all the time."

Aside from Mandy's official website, mandymoore.com, there are over a hundred unofficial ones!

ON THE TUBE

You can also keep up by watching her videos (over and over). To make sure they're always on, call MTV's *TRL* (1-800-342-5688) Monday to Friday 3:30 — 4:30 (EST). You might even get to chat with her in person!

SNAIL MAIL

If you want to mail something to Mandy, send it to this address:

Mandy Moore
c/o Storefront Entertainment
7060 Hollywood Blvd #1118
Los Angeles, CA 90029

All this success and Mandy still finds it hard to believe: "I almost don't want it to sink in, because I don't ever want to take it for granted."

No question, this is a Mandy Millennium. TV and movie appearances, product endorsements, MTV, the Internet and beyond — Mandy will be there. But in the end, the most important thing to Mandy will always be her music. She says, "Truthfully, I want to be someone who is remembered. I want people to grow up with Mandy Moore. Many musicians today go off and do movies and forget their focus. I think that is great, just as long as they remember their heart is in music." There's no question where Mandy's heart is.

But Mandy still has a lot of new challenges ahead in the music industry. And knowing Mandy, she'll be facing every one of them with the same excitement she showed on *So Real*. Most important to her right now is her creative role on her next album titled, *I Wanna Be With You*: "On the next album, I want to write as many songs as I can and produce them, and executive produce the whole album." With Mandy's talent, there's no question her new album will be phenomenal. The only bad part will be . . . waiting for it to come out.

They key to success? Talent, drive, and knowing how to have fun.

ASK MANDY

Q: Down the road . . . what do you want to be doing?

A: Eventually, I want to be on Broadway, or star in movies, like Bette Midler does.